Piano Literature
of the 17th, 18th and 19th Centuries

Frances Clark ® LIBRARY FOR PIANO STUDENTS

Selected and Edited by Frances Clark, Louise Goss and Sam Holland

Cover Design: Debbie Johns

© 2003, 1956, 1957, 1958, 1974 Summy-Birchard Music
division of Summy-Birchard Inc.
All Rights Reserved   Printed in U.S.A.
ISBN: 0-87487-128-X

Summy-Birchard Inc.
exclusively distributed by
Warner Bros. Publications
15800 NW 48th Avenue
Miami, Florida 33014

PREFACE

The five volumes of the *Piano Literature* series (Books 2, 3, 4, 5, and 6) contain a selection of choice smaller works in original form by master composers of the seventeenth, eighteenth, and nineteenth centuries. Because there is almost no keyboard music by master composers easy enough for first-level students, Book 1 is a collection of folk songs and singing games in delightful piano arrangements.

The selections in Book 2 and the following volumes were carefully considered from the standpoint of difficulty, not only technically but musically. In each volume, our aim has been to include compositions of fairly uniform difficulty and only compositions that can be played beautifully by the average student at that level.

The series is planned to provide:
1) A thorough musical preparation for performance of the composers' major keyboard works through experience with representative smaller works at each of the five levels.
2) Experience in a variety of styles and forms and an understanding of the way these styles and forms have developed in the history of music.

All of the selections are presented in their original form. The fingerings are based on a study of the tempo and dynamics as well as ease of performance. We are aware that in many cases there may be more than one good way to finger a passage and recommend that students study the fingering from the standpoint of what best fits their own hands.

A glossary, containing definitions of all the musical terms used in the music and in the biographical notes, appears at the end of each book.

Frances Clark, Louise Goss and Sam Holland

Contents

Johann Sebastian Bach
1685–1750

Johann Sebastian Bach was the greatest member of a famous musical family. The Bachs had been well-known musicians in Germany for two centuries before Johann Sebastian was born, and four of his sons—Carl Philipp Emanuel, Johann Christian, Johann Christoph, and Wilhelm Friedemann—contributed to the family's fame in the eighteenth century.

For almost one hundred years after Bach's death, his music was practically unknown. Then a German musician of the nineteenth century, Felix Mendelssohn, rediscovered some of his compositions and began to perform them in public. Ever since that time, people have recognized Bach's music as among the greatest and most beautiful ever written.

Bach's compositions are almost the last and perhaps the greatest music of the baroque period, an era in music history that began about 1600. In fact, Bach's compositions mark such a climax of this style that we frequently use the year of his death, 1750, as a convenient date for the end of the baroque period in music.

The baroque period saw the rise of many of the kinds of music still written today: opera, oratorio, sonata, suite, and concerto. During this period, each country contributed special features of musical style. The Italians developed long, arching, tuneful vocal melodies and an orchestral style of great power and rhythmic drive. French composers specialized in elegant harpsichord music, in which simple melodies were decorated with many ornaments. The Germans contributed keyboard compositions, especially for organ, of great brilliance and speed; their specialty was contrapuntal music, of which the fugue was a highlight.

As a composer, Bach borrowed from almost every style popular in the baroque period. One of the most important parts of his music is that which he wrote for clavier. The pieces that follow were composed for harpsichord or clavichord, early forerunners of the piano. Even though the piano was invented in Bach's lifetime (1709), he played the new instrument only a few times and never composed any music for it. Today, we play his clavier music on the piano.

The preludes in this collection come from two sets of *Little Preludes and Fugues,* which Bach composed for students.

Prelude in C Major

From *Six Small Preludes, BWV Anh. 939*

Johann Sebastian Bach

Prelude in C Major

From *Notebook for Wilhelm Friedeman, BWV Anh. 924*

Johann Sebastian Bach

Prelude in F Major

From *Notebook for Wilhelm Friedeman, BWV Anh.927*

Johann Sebastian Bach

8

George Frideric Handel
1685–1759

George Frideric Handel was born in Halle, Saxony, less than a month before Bach was born in Eisenach. Handel's father was a barber, who later became surgeon to the Prince of Saxe-Magdeburg at Weissenfels.

Father Handel wanted his son to become a lawyer or practical businessman and at first opposed his interest in music. Despite his father's opposition, George Frideric secretly taught himself to play the harpsichord.

At the age of seven, Handel often went with his father on visits to Weissenfels, where he had a chance to try the prince's chapel organ. On one visit, the prince heard him play and urged that Handel be given a musical education.

With this encouragement, Handel's father arranged to have his son study with Zachau, the organist at Halle. For a number of years, Handel devoted himself to the study of theory, harmony, oboe, violin, harpsichord and organ. For a time, he was a law student at the University of Halle, but he soon went to Hamburg as a violinist for the Hamburg opera. There his first two operas were written and produced.

As a young man, Handel visited the music centers of Italy, where he met leading musicians of that country (among them Domenico Scarlatti) and produced his first operas in Italian style. Later, he became music director for the Elector of Hanover and even visited England, where his operas met with great success.

Eventually, Handel settled permanently in England and became a British subject. In London, he was made director of the new Royal Academy of Music, for which he composed many successful operas. Later, he wrote oratorios with equal success. In 1741, he was invited to Ireland, where his most famous oratorio, *Messiah,* was first produced.

When he was an old man, Handel's health and sight began to fail. But even after he became totally blind, he continued to compose. He died at the age of 74 and was buried with high honors at Westminster Abbey.

Although most of Handel's keyboard music was for organ, he composed three volumes of suites for harpsichord and some miscellaneous harpsichord pieces. The courante, sonatina, and sarabande included here are among the few short, separate keyboard pieces he composed.

Courante

From *Pieces pour le clavecin: III, No. 7*

George Frideric Handel

Sarabande

Suite from *Suites de Pieces: II, No. 4*

George Frideric Handel

0128S

Sonatina

From *Pieces pour le clavecin: III, No. 10*

George Frideric Handel

Domenico Scarlatti
1685–1757

*T*hree of the greatest composers of the baroque period—Johann Sebastian Bach, George Frideric Handel, and Domenico Scarlatti—were born in 1685.

Scarlatti was born in Italy in the city of Naples, where his father, Alessandro Scarlatti, was one of the most important early opera composers. As a boy, Domenico studied harpsichord, organ, and composition with his father and, at the age of 16, was appointed organist and composer for the royal chapel in Naples.

As a young man, Scarlatti had a number of church positions, including the post as music director of St. Peter's in Rome. While Queen Maria Casimira of Poland was living in Rome, he was her music director and later he went to Lisbon, where he became music teacher at the royal court. When his pupil Maria Barbara became Queen of Spain, she made Scarlatti court composer, a post he held for the rest of his life.

Scarlatti was one of the most gifted harpsichord players of his day. When he and Handel were both 24 years old, they had a friendly music contest in Rome. Handel was judged the better organist, but as harpsichordists they were voted equal.

Although he began his career as a composer of operas, after settling in Spain, Scarlatti wrote primarily for the harpsichord. He composed more than six hundred harpsichord pieces, five hundred of which he called "exercises" or "sonatas." Almost all of these sonatas, two of which follow, are made up of one short movement in two equal parts.

Sonata in D Minor
K. 32

Domenico Scarlatti

Moderato

Sonata in G Major

K. 431

Domenico Scarlatti

Carl Philipp Emanuel Bach
1714–1788

One of the most important composers between Johann Sebastian Bach and Franz Joseph Haydn was Bach's second son, Carl Philipp Emanuel. This famous son, who was born in Weimar in 1714, took music lessons from his father and learned to play the organ, harpsichord, and clavichord and to compose. At the University of Frankfurt, he studied philosophy and law but soon gave them up in order to devote all of his time to music.

For nearly thirty years, Philipp Emanuel lived in Berlin, where he was a musician in the court of King Frederick the Great. Later in his life, Philipp Emanuel moved to Hamburg, where he became music director of the principal churches.

Philipp Emanuel was one of the most important German composers and musicians of the mid-eighteenth century. In fact, to his contemporaries, the name "Bach" meant Carl Philipp Emanuel, not his father, Johann Sebastian. In speaking of Philipp Emanuel's importance to eighteenth-century music, Mozart said: "He is the father, we are the children."

Philipp Emanuel was born toward the end of the Baroque period. His early music lessons from his father were based on baroque music, and he learned to compose in baroque style. But as he grew older, he became an important composer in the pre-classic style of his own generation. In fact, his music may be said to mark the change from baroque musical style to the style of the classic period.

Philipp Emanuel had been brought up on the harpsichord and clavichord, but as a young man at the Court of Frederick the Great, he began to play the piano. He became one of the finest pianists of his time and one of the leading early composers of piano music. He wrote more than two hundred short pieces—such as the Allegro, Solfeggietto, and Fantasia—and many piano sonatas, which pianists and composers have been playing and studying ever since.

Allegro

Carl Philipp Emanuel Bach

Solfeggietto

Wot. X, No. 17

Carl Philipp Emanuel Bach

Fantasia
Wot. X, No. 117

Carl Philipp Emanuel Bach

(Franz) Joseph Haydn
1732–1809

*J*oseph Haydn was one of the outstanding composers of the eighteenth century. He was born a poor peasant boy in the village of Rohrau in Austria. As a choirboy in a church in Vienna, he learned to sing and to play the violin, harpsichord, clavichord, and organ and taught himself to compose.

As a man, he became music director for Prince Esterházy. On the Esterházy estate, Haydn was outside the brilliant musical world of nearby Vienna, but he had an excellent choir and orchestra to direct and an opportunity to experiment with many new musical ideas. For the prince's entertainment, he wrote symphonies, sonatas, chamber music, and choral music.

Haydn lived during an important period in the history of music. Mozart was his friend, Beethoven was his pupil, and many of the other musicians of the time were his acquaintances. Because so many great composers lived and worked in Vienna during this part of the eighteenth century, the period is sometimes referred to as the Viennese period. The years 1770–1825, in which most of the Viennese composers were writing, are generally called the classic period, because the music written then is in the style known as classic.

Classic-period music is marked by forms, which are very regular and clear. Its melodies are song-like and simple in design, its harmonies simple and generally straightforward, and its rhythms regular and frequently repeated. In addition, classic-period music seems to be calm and restrained in its emotional appeal.

Along with many other kinds of compositions, Haydn also wrote some separate minuets for piano, like the two given here. These were not composed to be danced but make use of the minuet form as the inspiration for a concert piece.

Minuet in C Major

Hob. IX: 8/1

Joseph Haydn

Trio

D.C. al Fine

Allegro Scherzando

Hob. III: 73/4

Franz Joseph Haydn

Wolfgang Amadeus Mozart
1756–1791

Mozart was one of the greatest composers and most remarkable musicians of all time. He began to compose when he was only five years old and while he was still a small child, played for kings and queens all over Europe. The most famous musicians of his time praised him and prophesied that he would become a great musician.

Mozart was the son of violinist and composer Leopold Mozart. Wolfgang was born in the city of Salzburg, where his father was a court musician for the archbishop. Leopold was his son's first teacher, and at the age of four, Wolfgang began to play the harpsichord and violin. At the age of six, he could also play the organ and piano and had begun to compose.

From that time on, he never stopped writing music. In the brief 35 years of his life, he wrote more than forty symphonies, many operas and operettas, concertos and sonatas for piano and other instruments, string quartets, and church music. In addition, he was one of the finest pianists of his period.

In the eighteenth century, most musicians were employed by a court or church. Court musicians in those days were treated as servants; they had to dress in servants' uniforms, eat with the servants, and enter and leave the palace through the servants' door. When Mozart worked for the Archbishop of Salzburg, he resented this treatment and found his position as a servant hard to endure. After he left Salzburg, he tried without success for several other positions and was finally forced to earn a living on his own as best he could. This makes him one of the first musicians who tried to earn a living without the patronage of church or court.

Mozart was another of the Viennese classic composers. He wrote in the classic style, which Haydn had done so much to develop. Although "Papa" Haydn, as Mozart called him, was old enough to be the younger composer's father, the two men became close friends. Mozart claimed he learned how to write string quartets from Haydn, and Haydn claimed that Mozart was the greatest musician he knew. Unlike Haydn, Mozart was not a musical "pioneer"—he did not introduce anything "new" to music. But he took the forms and styles of the men who had gone before him and brought them to the highest level of perfection.

The movements that follow come from a set of six Divertimentos, K. 439b, which Mozart composed for two clarinets and bassoon and which we have transcribed for piano.

Klavierstück
K. 33B

Wolfgang Amadeus Mozart

Andantino
K. 236 (588b)

Wolfgang Amadeus Mozart

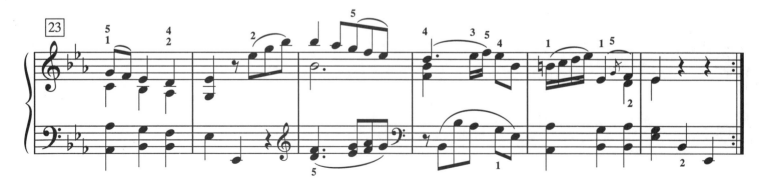

Rondo

Wolfgang Amadeus Mozart

Allegro

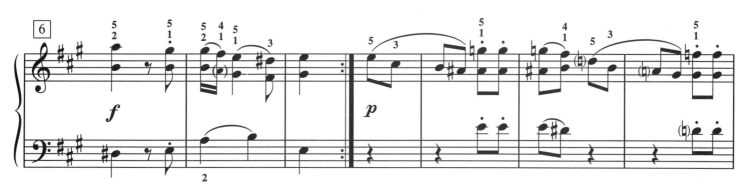

30

0128S

Ludwig van Beethoven
1770–1827

*L*ike Haydn, Ludwig van Beethoven rose from poor surroundings to become one of the greatest and best-known musicians of his time. He was born in the city of Bonn on the Rhine river in Germany, where his father and grandfather were musicians in the court of Clemens August, the Elector of Cologne. He had his first music lessons from his father and other members of the court orchestra.

Although Beethoven never had a real piano teacher, he became one of the most famous pianists of his day and one of the greatest composers of piano music in the eighteenth and nineteenth centuries. As a man, he lived in Vienna, where he knew Mozart and studied for a time with Haydn. After Mozart's death, be became the best-known pianist and extemporizer in the country.

When he was only 30 years old, he began to lose his hearing, and for the last years of his life he was tone deaf. But even when he could hear his music only inwardly, he continued to write greater and greater compositions—symphonies, overtures, string quartets, and a great deal of piano music. The *Six Variations on a Swiss Song* that follow make an ideal introduction to Beethoven's many sets of variations for piano. The dance is taken from a set of country dances.

As a young man in Bonn, Beethoven had been a court musician. But, like Mozart, he resented being treated as a servant. After he went to Vienna, he never again took a court or church position. Several wealthy men who admired his music helped support him, but he earned an adequate income by teaching, by giving piano concerts, and from his published music. Although Mozart had tried to earn a living without the support of the court, he died in poverty. Beethoven, on the other hand, lived successfully without court patronage and thus became one of the first independent professional musicians.

During Beethoven's lifetime, the classic style of Haydn and Mozart was gradually giving way to a new musical style, which has become known as romanticism. Beethoven's music reflects this change. He continued to write in the classic style using classic forms, yet at the same time his works served as the inspiration for a new kind of music, which Schubert, Schumann, and Chopin were soon to write. For this reason, Beethoven's music is seen as the bridge between two periods in music history, the point at which one musical style gives way to another.

Country Dance

WoO 15, No. 1

Ludwig van Beethoven

[Fine]

[D.C. al Fine]

Six Easy Variations
on a Swiss Song
WoO 64

Theme

Ludwig van Beethoven

Andante con moto

Var. I

Var. II

Var. III
Minore

Var. IV
Maggiore

Var. V

Var. VI

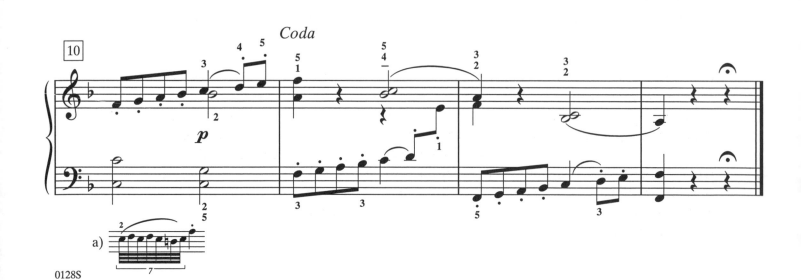

Franz Schubert
1797–1828

Franz Schubert was born in a suburb of Vienna, called Lichtenthal, where his father was a schoolteacher. The Schuberts were enthusiastic amateur musicians; Father Schubert was a good cellist, and the Schubert family string quartet was known all over Lichtenthal.

As a boy, Schubert studied music at the Royal Chapel Choir School in Vienna and took some lessons from the great composition teacher Salieri. As a young man, Schubert taught school with his father in Lichtenthal but soon gave up teaching in order to devote all of his time to composing. He never had a regular income and always had a hard time earning enough money for food and shelter. Two summers he taught music at the Esterházy Estate, where for many years Haydn had been music director.

Schubert lived only 31 years, but in that time he wrote an unbelievable amount of music—symphonies, string quartets, songs, and piano music. The piano compositions and songs are his greatest works. No composer wrote more easily than he. In his lifetime, he composed more than six hundred songs; 114 of them were written in one year, and he was known to compose as many as eight in one day. One of his greatest songs, "The Erlking," was written in 20 minutes. Although Schubert was not a gifted pianist, he wrote a great deal of beautiful piano music—hundreds of waltzes like those in this collection, many impromptus and *moments musicaux,* sonatas, and other kinds of compositions.

Schubert was born just before the beginning of the nineteenth century, and although he lived only one year after Beethoven, he was a younger man and a member of a different generation. Although both composers stood at the threshold of the romantic period, Schubert went further toward the new romantic style.

Composers of the romantic period were less concerned with form than classic composers and more concerned with expressing a mood. Romantic music is full of striking contrast; on one hand, it contains large, varied works of impressive grandeur, and on the other, delicate, miniature compositions, which create a single intimate mood. Romantic melodies are marked by similar contrasts: a quiet song-like melody will suddenly be interrupted by a fierce outburst, or a single melody will contain both very loud and very soft passages with constant variation between. Romantic harmonies are in general more complex and colorful than those of the classic period. Because Schubert's music contains many of these characteristics, he is considered one of the first romantic composers.

Écossaise

Franz Schubert

Three Waltzes

From *Thirty Six Waltzes, D. 365, Nos. 1, 2, 3*

I

Franz Schubert

II

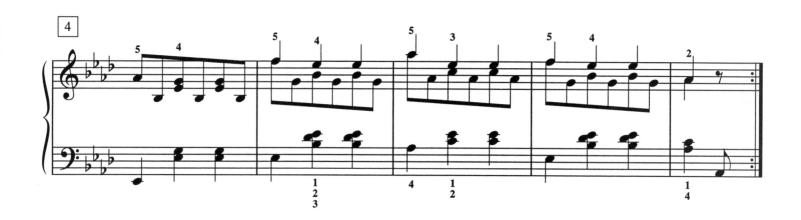

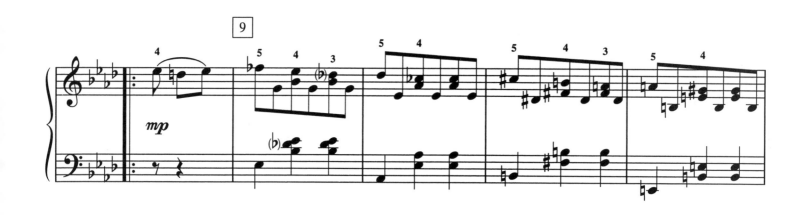

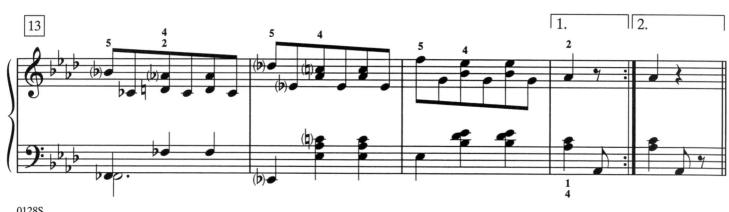

III

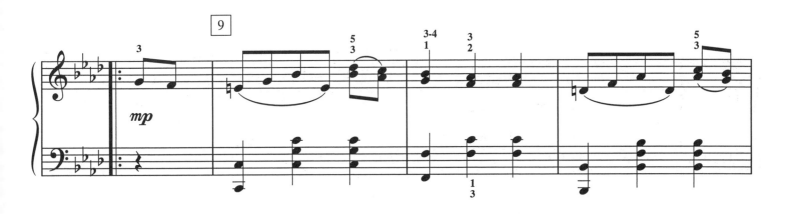

Robert Schumann
1810–1856

*A*fter the death of Beethoven and Schubert, Robert Schumann became the leader of the romantic movement in Germany. A composer and a music critic, he was one of the most important musicians of the nineteenth century.

Schumann was born in the city of Zwickau in Germany. His family loved music, and Schumann grew up in a musical and literary atmosphere.

As a young man, he planned to become a concert pianist and began to study piano with Friedrich Wieck in Leipzig. He invented a mechanical device to strengthen his weak fourth finger and used it so much that he crippled his hand. After he had to give up a concert career, he began to study composing and wrote symphonies, chamber music, songs, and piano compositions. His wife, Clara, who became one of the finest women pianists of her time, often gave concerts of his piano music.

Schumann had always been interested in literature as well as in music, and during much of his life, he not only composed music but also wrote articles about the music and musicians of his day. For many years, he lived in Leipzig, a great musical center of the time, where other composers (among them Mendelssohn, Liszt, and Brahms) were his friends and associates. In order to explain his own music and the music of his friends, Schumann founded a musical magazine and for ten years was its editor.

In this magazine, he wrote articles about the new composers and their music, defending those who tried new ways and criticizing those who clung to the style of the past. He explained the romantic movement and its music to his readers and helped them understand and love it. In this way, he became the real leader of the romantic movement in Germany, carrying on the work that Beethoven and Schubert had started.

His piano music is typically romantic. Many of his pieces are little fragments, with personal and expressive melodies, rich and colorful harmonies, and lively changing rhythms. In addition to many difficult piano compositions, Schumann wrote an entire album of beautiful short pieces just for students. He called it *Album for the Young*; the music in this album is as lovely and interesting as anything he wrote. The pieces that follow are taken from this collection and from a collection called *Autumn Leaves*.

Norse Song

From *Album for the Young,* Op. 68

Robert Schumann

Like a folk song

0128S

Waltz

From *Album Leaves,* Op. 124

Robert Schumann

Lively

With Pedal

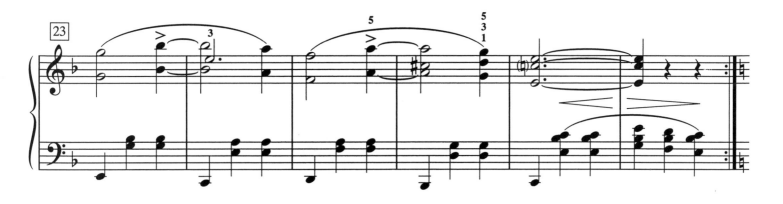

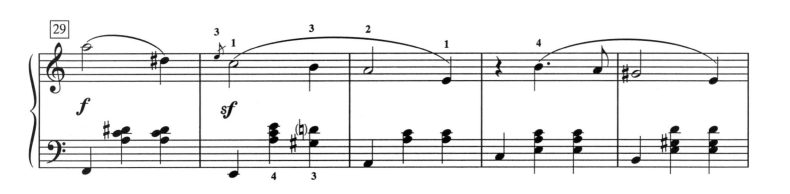

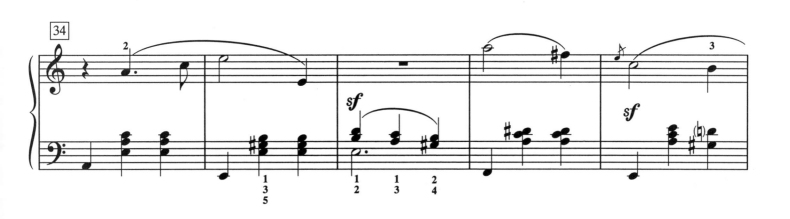

Peter Ilyitch Tchaikovsky
1840–1893

Tchaikovsky lived in Russia in the days of the czars. When he was a young man, a group of amateur Russian musicians known as "The Five" were making a reputation as Russia's first important composers. These men—Moussorgsky, Borodin, Rimsky-Korsakoff, Cui, and Balakirev—have been called Russian nationalists because they were interested in writing music that would sound Russian and would express Russian national feelings.

Despite their importance to Russian music, "The Five" were largely untrained amateurs technically unequipped to lead Russian music into new paths. Tchaikovsky became Russia's first professional composer, the first whose thorough musical training lifted him out of the amateur class and equipped him for a musical career. Although his music has many Russian characteristics, Tchaikovsky had a typical German romantic background and was more interested in the beauty and sentimentality of his music than in its Russian sound.

Tchaikovsky studied at the Conservatory of Music in St. Petersburg and later became a professor of harmony at a new conservatory in Moscow. Most of his life, however, he spent composing symphonies, symphonic poems, ballets, operas, and piano music.

He had a wealthy friend, Madame von Meck, who was so interested in his music that she became his patron and helped support him all of his life. Although these two friends agreed never to meet, they became very closely associated through their letters, and many of Tchaikovsky's best compositions were written for Madame von Meck.

Tchaikovsky lived almost to the end of the nineteenth century, and his music represents the height of the romantic period. It is filled with long beautiful melodies, full harmonies, and rich orchestral colors. It is sentimental music and expresses emotions that are easy to grasp and to which we respond quickly. It is often called "pathetic" music because the emotions it expresses are so often those of a person who seems to enjoy feeling sorry for himself.

However, not all of Tchaikovsky's music is "pathetic." Much of it, like *The Nutcracker,* is bright, tuneful, and gay. This is particularly true of the piano pieces in his *Album for the Young,* from which "Morning Prayer" and "The Witch" are taken.

Morning Prayer

From *Album for the Young,* Op. 39

Peter Ilyitch Tchaikovsky

The Witch

From *Album for the Young*, Op. 39

Peter Ilyitch Tchaikovsky

Edvard Grieg
1843–1907

*E*dvard Grieg was born in Bergen, Norway, in the middle of the nineteenth century. His mother, a gifted pianist, was his first music teacher.

At the age of 15, he went to Germany and enrolled at the Conservatory of Music in Leipzig, where he studied harmony, counterpoint, composition, and piano.

As a man, Grieg was active in many musical societies in Norway. He traveled widely as a concert artist, was for a time the conductor of the Philharmonic Society, taught piano and composition, and was constantly composing. The Norwegian government eventually gave him a lifetime income so that he could devote all of his time to composition.

As a composer, Grieg was influenced by the German romanticists Schumann and Mendelssohn. Though his music is romantic in style, he lived so near the end of the nineteenth century and the whole romantic movement that he is classed as a late-romantic composer. In his music and the music of other late nineteenth- and early twentieth-century composers, the romantic movement was gradually giving way to a new style called modern music.

In addition to its romantic style, Grieg's music is very Scandinavian in spirit. When the composer was 21, he became seriously interested in Norwegian folk music and from that time on used national themes and ideas as a main source of his style. In addition, he joined other composers in founding a society for the promotion of Scandinavian music.

Grieg wrote violin sonatas, chamber music, a little orchestral music, piano compositions, and songs. The piano music includes one famous concerto and many shorter compositions. These short pieces are somewhat like the brief descriptive pieces that Schumann and Chopin wrote—miniature tone-paintings in which a simple, clear-cut mood is presented through lyric melodies and rich harmonies. Grieg collected some of these miniatures into sets called *Lyric Pieces* and *Norwegian Folk Songs and Dances,* from which the following selections are taken.

Song of the Suitor

From *Norwegian Folk Songs and Dances,* Op. 17

Edvard Grieg

Watchman's Song

From *Lyric Pieces,* Op. 12
(Composed after a performance of Shakespeare's *Macbeth*)

Edvard Grieg

Molto andante e semplice

Intermezzo (Spirits of the night)

0128S

Hero's Song

From *Norwegian Folk Songs and Dances*, Op. 17

Con moto ma un poco maestoso

Edvard Grieg

Edward MacDowell
1861–1908

*E*dward MacDowell was one of America's first great composers. Most of his musical training took place in Europe, but as a young man he returned to his native country. Here he became one of the most unique composers America had produced to date. Although he lived into the twentieth century, he, like Grieg, was part of the romantic movement and can be classed as a late-romantic composer.

MacDowell was born in New York City in 1861. When he was eight, he began to study piano with leading teachers in New York and at the age of 15 went to Paris and enrolled in the Paris Conservatory. Later he studied in Germany, where Joachim Raff was his composition teacher.

While MacDowell was living in Germany, he met and played for the great pianist-composer Franz Liszt. Liszt was impressed with the young composer's ability and helped him get his first compositions published.

MacDowell held several teaching positions in Germany and then, in 1887, returned to America. At the age of 26, he settled in Boston, where for eight years he was active as a concert pianist, piano teacher, and composer. In 1896, he became head of the new music department at Columbia University, where he taught until 1904.

Although MacDowell was highly respected as a music educator, his lasting reputation is as a composer. He wrote several orchestral works, many songs, and a large amount of piano music, which place him among America's leading composers. His piano compositions include two concertos, four sonatas, and many short sketches, which were published in a number of albums. "To a Wild Rose" and "From an Indian Lodge" are taken from a famous collection called *Woodland Sketches*.

To A Wild Rose

From *Woodland Sketches,* Op. 51

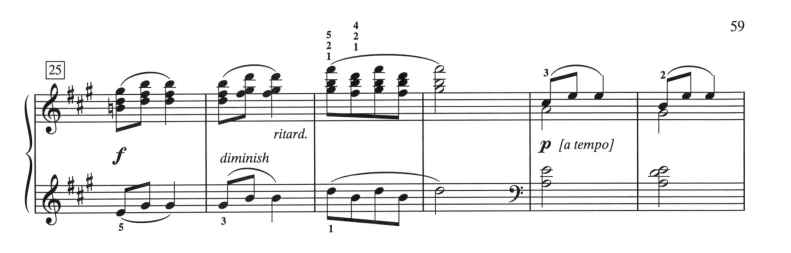

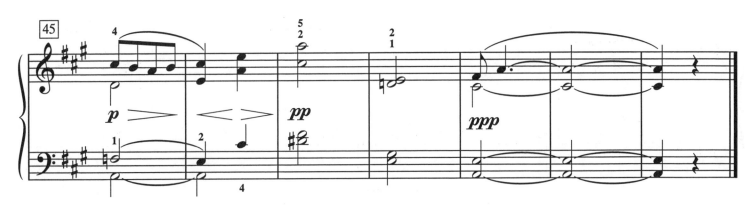

From an Indian Lodge

From *Woodland Sketches,* Op. 51

Sternly, with great emphasis

Edward MacDowell

Glossary

a tempo. In time; indicates a return to the original tempo after a ritardando or accelerando.

accelerando. (accel.) Getting gradually faster.

accent. (>) A sudden stress or emphasis of one tone that makes it stand out from others.

accompaniment. The part that provides musical background, as when a pianist accompanies a singer.

ad libitum. (ad lib.) An indication that gives the performer the privilege of varying slightly from strict tempo.

adagio. Slow tempo; a slow movement.

air. A short song, melody, or tune with or without words.

alla breve. (¢) A tempo indication for 2/2 time.

allegretto. Light and cheerful but not as quick as allegro.

allegro. Quick, lively; usually cheerful.

allegro di giusto. Quick; with emphasis on exact and steady time.

andante. A tempo between allegretto and adagio; flowing easily and gracefully.

animato. Animated; with life and spirit.

andantino. A little quicker than andante.

appoggiatura. An extra note added above or below a melody note; it is written before the beat like this:

but played on the beat like this:

baroque period. The period in music history from about 1600 to 1750.

bourrée. A rapid French dance in 2/4, 4/4, 2/2, or ¢ time.

cantabile. In a singing manner.

chamber music. Instrumental music performed by one player to each part; different from orchestral music in which there are many players to each part.

classic period. The period in music history from about 1750 to 1825.

clavichord. The earliest type of stringed keyboard instrument; a forerunner of the piano.

clavier. Any stringed keyboard instrument.

coda. A few measures added to the end of a composition to make a more effective conclusion.

commodo. Quietly, easily, with composure.

con brio. With spirit.

con fuoco. With fire.

con moto. With motion.

concerto. A piece of music for a solo player accompanied by an orchestra; usually in three movements.

contrapuntal. See counterpoint.

contredanse. A popular French dance of the eighteenth century made up of several eight-measure sections. In the dance itself, two couples face each other and dance against (contre) each other in a variety of steps.

counterpoint. The term is derived from the Latin *punctus contra punctum,* which means "note against note." Properly interpreted, this means notes against notes, or melodies against melodies, hence the combination in music of lines or parts that have melodic significance. In contrapuntal music, melody is supported by other melodies, whereas in harmonic music melody is supported by chords.

courante (or corrente). A dance that became one of the standard movements in seventeenth-century suites; in moderate 3/2 or 6/4 time.

crescendo. (cresc.) —————— Getting gradually louder.

da capo al fine. (D. C. al fine) An indication that means to repeat the piece from the beginning and end at the place marked *fine*.

decrescendo. (decresc.) —————— Getting gradually softer.

diminuendo. (dimin. or dim.) Getting gradually softer.

dolce. Sweet and soft.

doloroso. Sad.

e. And.

écossaise. A Scottish dance in quick 2/4 time.

extemporize. To make up music as one goes along rather than to read music or to play music from memory.

fantasia. Literally, fancy, imagination, caprice; hence a kind of music in which the composer gives free scope to his ideas without regard to restrictions in form.

fermata. (⌢) A pause or hold. The sign appears over the note or rest that is to be sustained.

fine. The end.

forte. *(f)* Loud.

fortissimo. *(ff)* Very loud.

fugue. A form of imitative counterpoint based on a short melody (called the subject) that is stated at the beginning in one voice or part and then imitated by the other voices or parts in quick succession.

gigue. A rapid dance in 6/8 or 6/4 time; often used as the final movement in seventeenth- and eighteenth-century suites.

giocoso. Playful.

grace note. An extra note added above or below the written note:

**In music from Bach through Beethoven, the grace note is played very quickly at the beginning of the beat on the beat; after Beethoven, it is generally played as quickly as possible just before the beat.

grazioso. Graceful.

harmony. In general, any simultaneous combination of sounds, hence means "chord." Harmony also refers to successions of chords and the relationships between them, thus the chordal structure of music.

harpsichord. The keyboard instrument most popular before the piano was invented. The harpsichord tone is made by the action of tiny picks that pluck the strings, whereas the piano tone is made by the action of hammers that strike the strings.

impromptu. A name used as a fanciful designation for nineteenth-century character pieces for piano. The best-known examples are Schubert's Impromptus, Op. 90 and Op. 142.

improvise. To make up music as one goes along rather than to read music or to play music from memory.

in modo popolare. In popular style.

K. See Köchel.

Köchel. (In full, Köchel-Verzeichnis.) The chronological list of all the works of Mozart, which was made by Ludwig von Köchel.

L. See Longo.

ländler. Country dances.

legato. To be played as smoothly as possible, without any break between notes.

leggiero. Light, swift, delicate.

lento. Slow.

Longo. The catalogue of Domenico Scarlatti's harpsichord music, which was made by Alessandro Longo, who edited and published Scarlatti's complete keyboard works.

maestoso. Majestic, stately, dignified.

maggiore. Major.

marcato. Emphasize.

meno mosso. Less quickly.

minore. Minor

minuet. A moderately slow, stately dance in 3/4 time.

minuetto da capo. An indication, generally found after the trio section of a minuet and trio, which means to repeat the minuet from its beginning.

moderato. In moderate tempo.

molto. Very.

moments musicaux. A name, used particularly by Schubert, for lyrical character pieces for piano in romantic style.

mordent. An ornament consisting of alternation between the written note and the note immediately below, written:

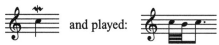

and played:

movement. A separate section of a longer work such as a sonata or symphony.

musette. Literally means bagpipe; sometimes refers to a composition, usually dance-like, with a droning accompaniment.

number. (No.) An individual piece, several of which make up a work or opus.

opus. (Op.) Work; used by composers to show in what order their works were written.

oratorio. A large work for vocal soloists, chorus, and orchestra based on a religious text arranged like a drama; unlike opera, however, oratorio is not presented with costumes, scenery, or stage action.

overture. An introductory piece played before an opera or play or as the first movement of a work such as the suite. The concert overture of the nineteenth century is an independent orchestral composition written along the same lines as the opera overture.

pianissimo. *(pp)* Very soft.

piano. *(p)* Soft.

poco. A little.

poco a poco. Little by little.

piu. More.

prelude. Properly, a piece of music designed to be played as an introduction. In the seventeenth and eighteenth centuries, often the first movement of a suite; sometimes a piece combined with a fugue. In the nineteenth century, the prelude became a pianistic character piece.

presto. Quickly, rapidly.

quadrille. A French dance, the music for which was often chosen from popular tunes.

rallentando. (rall.) Getting gradually slower.

ritardando. (ritard. or rit.) Getting gradually slower.

ritenuto. Detained, slower, held back.

robusto. Vigorous, bold.

romantic period. The period in music history from about 1825 to 1900.

romanze. A slow lyric instrumental piece.

rondo. The form often used in sonatas, symphonies, and concertos for the last movement; usually joyful or playful in mood. One main theme or melody returns again and again, interrupted by new themes: A-B-A-C-A-D-A, etc.

scherzo. Literally, a jest. A piece of music of a playful character, generally in fast tempo and in 3/4 or 6/8 time. In the early nineteenth century, the scherzo replaced the minuet as one of the movements of the sonata or symphony.

semplice. Simple.

sempre. Always.

sempre staccato il basso. The bass always distinct and detached.

sforzando. (sf. or sfz.) A sudden or strong accent on a single note or chord.

solfeggietto. Little study.

sonata. A composition for a solo instrument (piano, violin with piano accompaniment, etc.) in three or four movements, generally in this order: allegro, adagio, scherzo (or minuet), allegro.

sonatina. A little sonata, with fewer and shorter movements. The form of the first movement often differs from the form of the first movement of the sonata in that recapitulation immediately follows exposition without any development.

sostenuto. Sustaining the tone; keeping the notes sounding their full duration.

spiritoso. Spirited.

staccato. Detached; in performance, staccato notes are given half their written value or less.

string quartet. A chamber music group made up of four players: first violin, second violin, viola, and cello; "string quartet" is also used to mean the music written for such a group.

suite. An instrumental work made up of several dance movements all in the same key.

symphonic poem. A one-movement work for symphony orchestra inspired by a story, painting, or poem.

symphony. A large work for orchestra, generally in four movements.

tema. Theme.

tempo di marcia. March time.

tempo primo. First time. Used after a change in tempo to indicate a return to the original tempo.

tranquillo. Calmness, quietness.

trill. (tr.) Extra, ornamental notes, in the baroque and classic periods written: [musical notation] and played: [musical notation] in romantic and modern music, written: [musical notation] and played: [musical notation]

trio. A composition for three voices or instruments; also a contrasting second movement or part in compositions like the minuet, march, and gavotte.

turn. (∾) an ornament, generally written: [musical notation] and played: [musical notation] Sometimes the sign is placed to the right of the written note: [musical notation] In this case the main note is sounded first: [musical notation]

un poco piu lento. A little more slowly.

variations. A musical composition made up of one theme played over and over, each time varied or changed in a different way.

vivace. Animated, quick, lively.

vivo. Animated, lively, brisk.